Winter

Light

Winter Light

A

Christian's Search

for Humility

Bruce Ray Smith

Winter Light

Published by:

Kalos Press, an imprint of Doulos Resources, 195 Mack Edwards Drive, Oakland, TN 38060, USA; PHONE: (901) 451-0356; WEBSITE: www.doulosresources.org.

Please address all questions about rights and reproduction to Doulos Resources, 195 Mack Edwards Drive, Oakland, TN 38060, USA; PHONE: (901) 451-0356; E-MAIL: info@doulosresources.org.

Published 2011

Printed in the United States of America by Ingram/Lightning Source

ISBNs:

978-0-9828715-8-4 (trade paperback edition)
978-0-9828715-9-1 (electronic/digital editions)

Library of Congress Catalogue Number: 2011928886

Cover credits:

Main photo by Inga Ropsa (http://www.inga-design.com)
Author photo by Sylvester Jacobs
Cover design by David Bedsole

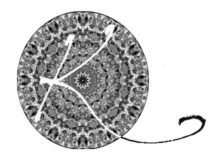

For Jane

ove means to learn to look at yourself
The way one looks at distant things
For you are only one thing among many.
And whoever sees that way heals his heart,
Without knowing it, from various ills . . .

~ Czesław Miłosz, "Love"

CONTENTS

FOREWORD

Voluntours Day?

*I*n 2006, Bruce Ray Smith lost a job he was good at. For six years he had been teaching English and creative writing at a Catholic prep school for girls, where he was beloved by his students and well-regarded by his peers. By all counts, it was a good fit, but a new administration was looking for something different.

Bruce was devastated. It was tempting for him to take refuge in cynicism. Fighting against this, he turned to writing—not about cynicism, but something deeper, something more pervasive and troubling. He began to write about human pride, including his own. He wanted to know the meaning of humility. To do this well requires a level of candor so unnerving that few dare attempt it.

Halfway through *Winter Light*, the reader may think, "Why does this poor fellow do this to himself?" What is he trying to accomplish?" I have been Bruce's brother, pastor, and friend for the past sixteen years. We have eaten, prayed, watched baseball together. What the reader needs to know is that Bruce Ray Smith takes what is wrong with the world, hard, and what is wrong with himself, harder still. This is why he writes as he does.

Bruce has something in common with St. Augustine, who once quipped to a friend in a letter, "I am the sort of man who writes to make progress, and who makes progress—by writing." The book in your hands is one man's anguished longing for something more of his Lord, and of his Lord's internal rest. Bruce craves the rest and freedom that comes from knowing who he is, in relation to his Father in heaven and to the precious but desperately fallen people around him.

Not since reading Dietrich Bonhoeffer's remarkable poem, "Who Am I?" many years ago, have I felt so invited into the inner life of another man. I wouldn't call it comfortable, because *Winter Light* is not. It stings. It is an exposé. Admissions abound that put every honest heart at risk. I found myself saying with alarming frequency, "Yes, exactly! This is my experience too." If humility is seeing ourselves as we really are, then such stinging is salutary and essential. It is the Master's word bearing fruit in us, as he promised: "Whoever loses his life for me and the gospel will save it."

Bruce and his wife Jane chose many years ago to live in a part of St. Louis called Old North. Their home is just a stone's throw from Interstate 70, which slices through their neighborhood, cutting them off from Broadway and the Mississippi River several blocks to the east. The people who live there are colorful. Many are imaginative and ambitious homesteaders. Fresh tuck-pointing marks late nineteenth-century renovated dwellings; wrought iron fences and brick sidewalks dot the landscape. New commercial enterprises have sprung up.

It can be an intriguing place to live and even to visit, but can also try the patience of the soul. Absentee owners abandon their properties to weeds and vandals. Buildings gutted by fire are exposed for years to the elements. Like other urban neighborhoods, it can be loud, sometimes dangerous. These things have vexed Bruce for years, but Old North is his home. It has shaped, tested, and enriched him.

Years ago, Bruce invited me to go fishing with him on a lake in Illinois. I paddled. Bruce fished. From what I remember, it was a good day for the fish— but we salvaged the time with conversation and not a few laughs in an otherwise tranquil place. We could have talked about pride and humility, but we didn't. Most people don't when they go fishing.

It did not occur to me at the time that Bruce was a proud man. Did he hide it well, or was he more humble, then? Has a bit more humility been wrung out of his soul in the years since we unstrapped his canoe from the roof racks of his Toyota? Most of us who know Bruce don't think of him as a proud man. But he must know, for as the Scripture says, "Who knows the thoughts of a man except the spirit within him?" (I Corinthians 2:11)

We should let Bruce speak of what he knows. He wants to speak of it. He is writing for his progress. He is also writing for ours.

There is a great deal at stake. This book, especially the parts that sting, has the potential to change us. In the final analysis, as valuable as character is for every generation, it is not humility that we are so hungering and thirsting for. As Bruce puts it in these pages, "I want more. I want to *live in* Him . . . I want humility because I want much more."

~ Kurt Lutjens

1

SOMETHING

HAS HAPPENED

Something has happened to me.

I overhear myself, my own voice saying, "I don't know," and sometimes, "I was wrong."

Sometimes, I keep silence. Sometimes, now, I listen.

I have never listened.

~

*I*t began this way.

"I love you," I told God, "with all my heart, with all my soul—." I knew the rest, but stopped. I lived, had always lived, for no one but myself. My life belonged to no one but myself.

It took, I think, three days, and then I said, and meant it: "Do what you have to, Lord."

Do what you have to do to make me yours.

~

I had no doubt that God would act. He did. He took from me so many things, so suddenly, that I began a list of them: every position of authority. Beloved work, a beloved house. Diversions which consumed me. Everything I had thrown together, everything I had put to use, to construct what I called "my life."

~

My life. So I thought of it.

God himself was one of my troubles, one of my pleasures.

No more than one of the troubles, one of the pleasures of "my life."

⌒

God acts. I knew that he would act.

How nebulous that "spirituality" some think of when they think of God!

I knew that he would act.

⌒

3

 *G*od honors me. It is an honor to be taken seriously by God.

But he will be himself.

I was, I am, afraid of him. And right to be afraid.

⁓

I am not a humble man.

I want to know God, and despite my fear, to love him; I want to know my fellows and be known by them.

With little knowledge of myself and less of God, I say it: I desire the end of that which has defined me for myself, my pride.

⁓

I am "waiting on God."

I am waiting on God, who heard my prayer and took, at a stroke, my shelter, my identity, colleagues who loved me, students who admired me. And my livelihood, of course.

What now?

I will, at some point, lose my confidence and lose my way. I am afraid, not only of God but for my small, conventional mind, the meanness of my expectations. But I am not of two minds. I am not a worldly man. I do not know how, nor do I wish, to keep myself in comfort, come what may.

I do know what it means to suffer, what it means to be saved.

⁓

*T*his, then is my testament, my prayer against myself, against my assumption that nothing, no one, matters so much as I. I hope to find out what it means, in the language of my Lord, to die. What it means, perhaps, to live.

I call these jottings, in the fall of the year, at the fall of my earthly expectations, my Winter Journal.

Let winter come!

Let my change come.[i]

A PRAYER
AGAINST MYSELF

This afternoon, I was pressed for time, and other shoppers, most of them elderly, impeded my progress down the aisle at the grocery store. I was furious; they were, I was certain, at fault. This feeling of mine, this near-conviction, will not, of course, bear scrutiny. These old folk did their shopping exactly as I do, carefully, sometimes indecisively, sometimes unaware of their surroundings. They can, in fact, be charged with nothing but an unintentional obstruction of my will.

My will. And why is my will, I am driven to ask, more important than the wills of others?

The answer is, I'm afraid, "Because it's mine."

⌇

A Prayer Against Myself

*I*magine telling the truth: "I believe, in spite of the evidence—I have unshakeable faith—that I am, of every living creature, that One, the one who matters. What matters, in all the universe, is that my will be done." Though we live by this astonishing creed, we know better than to give it voice.

Pride will not bear scrutiny.

～

I am the kind of man who wants to know, and if possible, know why. But God draws a line and says, "No further."

"The secret things belong to the Lord our God," says Moses, "but those things which are revealed belong to us and to our children forever."[i]

Some things belong to God.

～

Like every proud man, I dislike proud people. What seems so right to think about myself seems silly, even dangerous, in my neighbor.

How ugly my neighbor's pride! I see how authority, no matter how small the office, goes to his head. I see in him how pride is father to presumption, envy, anger, every kind of ill spirit, even when the stakes are paltry.

⁓

With what ferocity I express—have always expressed—my checks and disappointments! I am furious at the three-car accident which halts my progress on the highway and the rock against which I stub my toe.

No one knows such intense, irrational frustration as that man who, scarcely aware of his assumptions, thinks himself a god.

⁓

A Prayer Against Myself

I cannot, at once, believe God and believe myself to be a god.

~

*D*are I trust myself? The very eyes through which I see are proud.

Is it possible to learn humility?

I dare trust God to guide my seeking and to change my heart.

~

*H*igh stakes.

To learn humility, it seems to me, might mean no less than to <u>discover what it is to be a man</u>.

What does it mean to be a man? Not to be nothing, not to be "a stone, a plant, a microbe,"[ii] not to be a god, but to be a man?

⌒

*T*here is that something I call *I,* which questions and assesses all it hears or reads—or remembers, dimly, from its dreams. That part of me, that voice which yields or refuses, says yes or no, which sometimes says no to its own desire—

There is that something. Someone who decides.

I am not quite at the mercy of my own disquiet, my confusion, my temptation to despair. I am, though I am not sure what I mean by it, myself.

And yet I pray against myself.

I pray against myself.

⌒

A Prayer Against Myself

I choose God: I declare myself.

I declare against myself.

~

Looking at my wife in lamplight, reading, I see at once that there is no way to account for it, this life I called my own.

Why am I here? Why she here, reading?

I have, I admit, allowed myself to be distracted. For years, I applied myself to pointless ambition, ephemeral desires, accumulating and discarding. I discarded without a thought, without regret, those things I longed for.

What things? Everything. Possessions, reputation, praise.

I was blind to the mystery of being, of being here, of being here and not elsewhere, of being here now.[iii]

Pride has kept me from wonder.

~

"*I* know what it means to suffer. What it means to be saved." I said it, but meant only this: I am a desperate man. I am not resourceful. It is not for form's sake that I pray.

I know from my experience, I know very well what the Psalmist means: "This poor man cried, and the Lord heard him, and saved him out of all his troubles."[iv]

How such a man can be proud I do not know.

⌒

I am ashamed to recognize myself in Bernard of Clairvaux's *Steps of Humility*. I am the man who, in conversation, does not desire to teach or learn, but rather to "know that you know that he knows."[v] I am that man who says to himself, "I am not as other men are."[vi]

⌒

A Prayer Against Myself

In conversation, when I do not understand, I let the matter pass. I do not care enough about my fellows. I do not care enough to interrupt.

～

Though I suffer from my isolation, I persist in it. I have not wanted to be known; I have hidden myself from others as best I could.

I understand, I have always understood, that to let myself be known puts my illusions about myself, puts everything I have invested in myself, in danger.

～

*T*hough I like to think myself broad-minded, a lover of knowledge, I am in fact penurious and small, an ignorant man.

I do not love learning, not really. Everything I learn proves yet again how much I do not know. I do not like to be reminded of my ignorance.

I prefer my illusions.

～

*A*s for the knowledge I possess, the things I preen myself for knowing, Proust is right: "What one knows does not belong to oneself."[vii]

～

A Prayer Against Myself

For most of my life, I now realize, I didn't want others to love me. I wanted them to be impressed by me. I didn't want to know others; I instinctively resisted being known. I was aware of my loneliness: pride made me suffer. I was willing to suffer.

⁓

"By the word of the Lord," says the Psalmist, "the heavens were made / And the host of them by the breath of his mouth." With the forming of a thought, the speaking of a word, God makes his desire reality: "For he spoke and it was done."[viii]

To be God: the thought exhilarates as it debases. To speak: to have. To form the desire and effect it. Never to know frustration.

I am spared much; I have not the means, and not quite the will, to aim for the kind of power some men pursue.

But, God help me, I am one of them.

That same infected blood flows in my veins.

⁓

I admit to envy, a sin I deprecate in others and to which I had thought myself immune. Envy is a strain, a virulent strain, of pride: I should not be so surprised, so mortified to find myself infected.

How can I admit that any other thinks, perceives, so well as I, that any other speaks so well as I? A proud man, seeing the truth about himself, is a bitter man.

He hates the one who threatens his illusion.

~

This evening, Jane and I meet with neighbors, all of them Christians, to pray about injustices in our corner of the North Side. Many of these neighbors are poor, ill-educated, ill-equipped to defend themselves, and I anticipate, unhappily, the role of defender, spokesman. In fact, several of them pray, unprompted, with such passion and eloquence, with such profound understanding of the Scriptures, that I am forced to confront, yet again, my pride.

I had—I confess it—preened myself upon my singularity. My neighbors, I discover, are as passionate, as eloquent, as knowledgeable as I.

A Prayer Against Myself

I feel foolish, ashamed, but also pleased, relieved. Pleased because I have more brothers and sisters than I knew. Pleased because God keeps and teaches them well. Relieved because this may be the first time God has answered my prayer for humility without having to hurt me.

⁓

"It is good for me that I have been afflicted," says the Psalmist.[ix]

I myself, in my small way, have been afflicted. I, too, am shown the tenderness of God.

I am not a masochist. I don't want God to hurt me.

I choose to trust him: I trust he takes no pleasure in my pain.

Do I welcome pain?

With trepidation. I am not a masochist.

⁓

"Let us make a name for ourselves," cried the builders of the tower of Babel, "lest we be scattered abroad over the face of the earth."[x]

Jesus understands them. He understands the nature of despair: "Those who do not gather with me," he declares, "are scattered abroad."[xi]

To Jerusalem, our Lord cries out, "How often I wanted to gather your children together, as a hen gathers her chicks under her wings, but you were not willing!"[xii]

Humility permits us to be gathered. Jesus gathers us: we are gathered together, every one who is willing, gathered together in him.

A Prayer Against Myself

When Jesus exclaims, "Assuredly, I say to you that it is hard for a rich man to enter the kingdom of heaven," his disciples respond with bewilderment: "Who then can be saved?" Our Lord's reply must be the theme of my Winter Journal: "With men this is impossible, but with God all things are possible."[xiii]

Do I pray against myself? Do I pray against my pride? Do I hope to find my way to humility? I have no power to change myself.

No power at all.

I know nothing but God's mercy. I want nothing but this gift, to know him.

∽

To know God.

I say it with fear—with fear and longing together—but I say it.

∽

I do not wish to be a parody of him whose name really is I Am. I have but an intermittent sense of who I am, but know what I cannot be: I am not that one who is, in himself, complete.

I was not meant to be alone, and he who persists in thinking he is God must be, in the end, alone. Like Richard III, he will find nothing but himself and no escape from self: "Richard loves Richard: that is, I am I."[xiv]

~

"*He* has scattered the proud in the imagination of their hearts," exclaims Mary, in the Song that bursts from her at her kinswoman Elizabeth's house.[xv] I understand her. Pride, my pride, is fundamentally an act of imagination: I imagine myself to be what I am not.

Pride divorces me from God and from my fellows; it makes certain I will have no reference point, no way of guessing what or who I am. I am scattered, as the builders of Babel, they who felt the urge to "make a name for themselves," were scattered.

What need God do, to punish me, but leave me to myself?

~

A Prayer Against Myself

This morning, at the breakfast table, I oppose, object, refuse. I am beside myself.

I am literally beside myself.

I sit beside myself and see myself at war against my wife, who loves me. I turn our quiet morning conversation, our little "talk," into a battleground.

I defend myself—I defend my indefensible assumptions about who I am. I insist, with anger, that Jane see me as I see myself.

As I have seen myself.

For I begin to see myself in a different light. The man Jane loves, I understand to my despair, is smaller, needier, more vulnerable, fearful, sinful than the man I thought myself to be.

～

I want to be cured of the ills with which my pride afflicts me. But even without them, even freed from isolation, contempt and self-contempt, I will be no better. I still won't know how to live; I won't know, not here nor in heaven, how to be until I learn who I am, who I am now and who God meant, means, me to be.

～

*E*ven as a child, I held myself separate from others and could not bear reproof. I did not know that I was proud; I am not sure I knew the word or the concept. But I was aware of myself, aware of my self-regard.

Even that much clarity may be rare. Pride is hard to detect because it is a way of seeing: a lens through which one sees. How then does one become aware of it?

I do not know.

Nonetheless, I am encouraged. I do identify my pride; I am dismayed by it.

A beginning.

~

"*D*isassembled man": Derek Walcott's phrase.[xvi] I myself am so in pieces, I must marvel at God: how does he find in me the semblance, even, of a person?

How can he know me?

How can it be that a man like me, so helpless, in such disarray, presumes?

In spite of me, in spite of my absurd assumptions about myself, my Lord pursues me, waits on me, attends me.

He knows, better than I do, who I am.

~

A Prayer Against Myself

I have no power to heal myself, no power to change my heart. No power against my pride.

What can I do but wait on God?

Very well.

I will wait on him.

CONFESSION

I am, I admit, afraid.

When I prayed "Do what you have to, Lord," he answered me.

God *answered* me.

He answered me, and thus I am afraid.

~

*G*od tells us that he is good, and I believe him. But he will do as he wills. Is he not God?

I do not define him or direct him; I cannot, in any way, control him.

When I say "my God," I speak the language of love.

He is himself.

~

Confession

If fear is the price of love, of life, I accept. I accept the conditions.

3

PITIFUL FLEDGLING

God makes me understand that I belong to him, that I am not my own.

Very well. I renounce my pride.

What next?

I wait. I am "waiting on God."

What do I want from him? A new way of seeing, of doing, without complacency, without despair.

I should like to find out what it means to be a man—not what I have meant by "be a man," but what God means by it. What does it mean to be a man? What does God mean by it?

I want to know I am a man, and to live as one: before God, before my fellows. With my fellows.

~

Pitiful Fledgling

I cannot define humility. I am not sure what it looks or feels like. I have never been humble.

Nor do I understand my desire for humility. I want that very thing I have always rejected, always found repugnant, always feared: to be not merely myself, but one among *others*.

～

*P*ride has kept me distant from others, distant from God. I know very little of this world of others, of anything or anyone beyond myself. I am given grace enough to hear in that word others an invitation: I am beckoned to the rail, offered a glimpse of a land I do not know.

～

Judging by family history, I have perhaps ten years of clarity left. I am tempted to ask, "Why now? Why reveal to me now, at this late date, my pride, your generosity of heart?" I am tempted to add, "To what end, Lord?"

I am thinking, I suppose, like a worldly man. Thinking, still, of accomplishments, "contributions." I suspect that in the days ahead, such notions will be shaken from me. Love is not a matter of accomplishments. And time, so important to us here, may have less meaning than we think.

God's mercy has never seemed so sweet to me. I desire, in these last years, to know God and be known by him. I don't want him to say, when I meet him, "I never knew you."[i]

∼

King Lear, awakened, or almost awakened from his pride, pursues, in a kind of fury, "unaccommodated man."[ii] If I am not a king, Lear wants to know, what am I? What does it mean to be a man and no more than a man?

I, like Lear, am driven to acknowledge my delusions. I want to know what I am not. If possible, I want to know what, who, I am.

The difference is that I am not merely driven. Why, I do not know. But God invites me.

⁓

How may I understand this God who knows me, knows what I am, and yet invites me?

⁓

Surely, all my striving to be an individual, all the rebellion and self-defense that attended it, has been unnecessary. We can't help being who we are. When I am able to see at all, I can see it, this remarkable coherence, in others: how beautiful, how original, how distinctly themselves they are!

I had been given already this precious self which I so anxiously looked about for, intermittently rediscovered, desperately advertised and angrily defended. Surely I can stop now, and learn to love God and my neighbors.

⁓

/f humility means understanding who I am in relation to God, and being one among others, it must also teach me to love myself rightly, "with charity instead of partiality."[iii] The way I have loved myself cannot be right: I spin from self-love to self-hatred to exhaustion to self-love. Whatever else humility means, it must mean the breaking of this cycle.

⁓

/t pleases me to think how often we bless, as we are blessed, unaware.[iv] How thoughtless, how prodigal, are my fellows! They offer me kindness without knowing they are kind; they smile at me for no reason; they open their hearts to me with staggering trust. And this is as it should be, this naiveté of theirs: "Do not let your left hand know what your right is doing."[v]

Humility is, in part, a matter of trust. We need not lay claim; we know the origin of all goodness.

We know who blesses and saves.

⁓

Pitiful Fledgling

I look over these last entries with surprise. I have spoken with an ease, enlightenment, assurance I do not, in any useful sense, possess. I believe in what I say, I am delighted to hear myself say it. But I do not trust myself. At the next sign of trouble, my friends will hear a different kind of talk from me.

Humility: a matter of thinking, of thinking rightly about ourselves, and something more. It is also, it must be, a matter of healing.

My Lord will have to heal my heart.

~

*T*his morning, after breakfast at a café in town, Jane and I went for a walk in the country. Autumn woods made us grave and lighthearted at once, the sky threatening and inviting by turn, the light now somber, now dancing, cypresses glowing green and tawny, sumac flaring from the undergrowth. Persimmons hung from a leafless tree like Christmas ornaments. We ate persimmons. After the last brief burst of rain, a painted lady butterfly ambled behind and before us like a friendly dog.

Why do I recount this day in my Winter Journal? I do not know. I am not a romantic; like most people of my time and place, I am not convinced that a flower "enjoys the air it breathes"[vi] or that such a setting brings one close to powers, good powers, inherent in the natural world.

This is what I know: that I was glad for things beyond my comprehension, happy with this woman I love, not so conscious of myself as I usually am.

To love and be loved. To be one among others. That much, yes.

⌇

One might say that to be humble is to make an accurate assessment of oneself. Is it not a simple matter? To know one is a man, that God is God. To know at least what one is not.

But no, it is more wonderful than that. Stranger, by far, than that.

We are invited. God invites us. We learn, in time, how much he loves us.

This proud man discovers that he is one among others; this woman, who can scarcely leave her bed for lack of self-regard, is raised gently by our Lord: "For whoever exalts himself will be humbled, and he who humbles himself will be exalted."[vii]

⌇

Pitiful Fledgling

The humble person does not know that he is humble. But this person I imagine—this person I would like to be—will recognize humility when he sees it in others.

⌒

It is true that, praying for humility, I pray against myself. I take up arms against myself.

But now I begin to doubt myself when I say "myself."

Am I sixty or sixteen? I ask myself what every adolescent asks: "Who am I?"

I do not question my uniqueness or my right to be. It is a question, rather, of imagination: I do not know, I cannot imagine, my self as God intended it, my self made whole.

I tried hard, for years, to define myself. Now I want God to show me who I am.

⌒

*W*henever I look back at my life, at yesterday or twenty-five years ago, I blush with embarrassment. Why? Why am I embarrassed by my life?

Am I ashamed? I have reason to be ashamed. I am not, have never been, compassionate, courageous, generous, merciful. More often, though, I am embarrassed at my failure to conceal myself, that unique, defenseless self my Lord so ardently pursues.

Perhaps self-consciousness is our inheritance—part of it—from the Fall. We are desperately concerned with appearances: if we fail to hide from God, we do our best to hide from each other. Like most people, I cannot bear to hear my recorded voice; I am embarrassed to be known, even to myself.

I should like to acknowledge this self, this pitiful fledgling. It will, perhaps, be an act of humility to accept him as he is.

⌒

*C*an anyone tell me who I am? He will have to do at least as well as Yeats, who assures Maud Gonne that "one man loved the pilgrim soul in you, / And loved the sorrows of your changing face."[viii]

Which is to say, I—any I at all—cannot be understood, cannot be known, at one glance, ten or twenty. Would you know me? Attend me, then, every minute of my life.

No one, not even I, can know me as God knows me.

~

*I*t is a check to pride to see how little I know myself. How far I am from understanding what or who I am! How far I am from grasping what it means to be "made in God's image."

I don't understand God.

How will I understand myself? *why should I?*

~

cannot imagine God. Though he seeks me out, though he loves me and teaches me to love him in turn; though he invites me, moves me, urges me to rest in his mercy, I cannot imagine him. Is it possible to know him? To know him in the way I hope, at least, to know my neighbors?

Most of what he does, he does beyond my sight and comprehension. I know something of his ways. I do know something of his love. I am glad to wait, to wait on him. Glad for what he sometimes shows me of himself.

"I greet him the days I meet him, and bless when I understand."[ix]

～

Pitiful Fledgling

I cannot imagine the Trinity, nor does the thought of it comfort me; it is, as the Psalmist says, "too high for me."[x] Yet the second person of the Trinity declares, "Take my yoke upon you and learn from me, for I am gentle and lowly in heart, and you will find rest for your souls."[xi]

That God himself should be, can be, "gentle and lowly in heart," is beyond my conceiving.

I do not know why God should tell us, in the Scriptures, things which are so clearly beyond our comprehension. I had meant to remind myself that Jesus came as a servant, came not for himself but for the sake of others. But I can only stammer, like Peter at the Transfiguration, "Master, it is good for us to be here."[xii]

Is it possible to understand humility?

Son of Man, Son of God, have mercy on me.

It suffices that I am loved.

⁓

I do not forget that God is God, that I myself am no more than a man. I am his creature.

When God speaks from the whirlwind, it does matter what he says to Job, but it matters more that he speaks at all, that he speaks to Job. If God terrifies this troubled man, he also honors him. Why should God speak to him?

"What is man, that you are mindful of him?" asks the Psalmist in wonder.[xiii] Job himself, in a different, angrier spirit, had asked of God, "What is man, that you should exalt him?"[xiv]

When God speaks, Job replies as he must: "I have uttered what I did not understand; / Things too wonderful for me, which I did not know."[xv] When God speaks, Job knows that he, Job, is a man, and that God is God. He knows.

~

I believe in God. I do not know why he allows what he appears, at least, to allow; why he neglects what he appears, at least, to neglect.

I do not wish, any more than others, to be taken for a fool.

Nonetheless, I believe him, sometimes against the evidence, or what seems the evidence, of my senses. I take sides against myself.

Sooner or later, a man like me, a man who wants to know, who insists on his right to know, must decide, once and for all, what it means to be a man, what it means to be humble, what it means to be proud.

Who does he think he is? In whom does he believe?

⁓

When God replies to Job, he has questions of his own. Who are you?

Who do you think you are?

But it is what God does not say that brings Job to his knees.

What the Voice from the whirlwind leaves unspoken: You do not have the *means* to understand.

Leave the things of God to God.

⁓

$\mathcal{M}$eanwhile, this same God persists with me.

He makes me see myself.

I too persist. I persist in my desire, and in my asking.

I begin to understand how little I know myself, how little I know my fellows. I begin to understand how much I do not know.

～

lonely

$\mathcal{B}$efore the Fall, we were creatures, and knew it; we loved God and knew he loved us. But being humble, we had no word for humility.

Because of pride, I know the word: *humility*. I know, too, the misery of separation from my God, and from my brothers and sisters.

I want to be restored. Even now, before this life is over, I want to see the signs of restoration.

～

41

Pitiful Fledgling

At my conversion, years ago, I prayed to God, gave myself to him, my "amen" followed by a vivid sense of his presence. Not before. After.[xvi]

Dare I say it? The things that matter are impossible.

My desire for humility is a cry of the heart. I do not understand the heart, nor do I understand that mysterious Spirit who gives words to my desire. This is what it feels like: out of the naught of self I cry to the one who creates out of nothingness, "Dear God, give me the mind and heart you love."

With God all things are possible.

Not a Virtue, but
a Recognition

Do we believe that knowledge is power? To think so, we must force ourselves to ignore the obvious. Let me revise it thus: if we desire nothing more than power over *other* others, then yes—knowledge will help us to that end. But the truth is that we have no power at all.

Do we believe that creatures like ourselves, who weaken and die against our wills, have power? Do we?

Humility is not, but should be, a simple matter of intelligence.

Not a Virtue, but a Recognition

There is, too, the problem of our moral choices.

Do we expect to be commended for our virtue? Jesus dispels that illusion: even on our best day, we have merely "done what was our duty to do."[i]

Our necessity is not to achieve, but to be restored; what we call virtue is the common currency of heaven.

Humility, then, is not a virtue, but a recognition.

⁓

Jesus promises to give me rest, but I am almost never at my ease. I am not at ease with myself, nor with others. I have never known "how to stay quietly in my room."[ii]

Why am I so desperate? Why are all of us desperate?

Like everyone since the Fall, I do my best to live without reference to others; I tried to live without reference to God.

I don't know how to live.

This, so far, is how I do it: from cry to cry.

⁓

I keep reassuring myself that I'm all right, that everything that isn't right can be set right.

I'm not all right. And I can't help myself.

～

Do I pray for humility? God's answer is to show me what I am.

I am helpless before my pride; I am helpless before my anger, which destroys my peace and the peace of others and condemns me to isolation.

Paul is right: I do those things I do not wish to do.

I can't control my own will.

～

Not a Virtue, but a Recognition

I don't know how to live.

This is what I know, at this point, about living: to do it one day at a time, to do it under God's mercy, expecting nothing at all.

My Lord will have to do the rest.

⌒

Why do we pretend to be at peace? Were we at peace, our Lord would not have said, would not have found it necessary to say to us, "Come to me, all you who labor and are heavy laden, and I will give you rest."[iii]

Perhaps I am wrong, but when I look at my neighbors, I see myself in them and cannot but conclude that Jesus, when he says, "all you," means "every one of you."

⌒

Why do we preach to or instruct each other in the guise of prayer? Do we not know who we are, or to whom we speak?

Why do we commend "the power of prayer"? It is not power we need, not knowledge, but God himself.

~

The Psalmist does not say, "I trust God to make me able, I trust God to help me do what I would do," but rather, "I trust in the mercy of God forever and ever."[iv]

~

Not a Virtue, but a Recognition

After several debilitating attacks, in 1889, Vincent Van Gogh wrote to his brother Theo, "I'm sure that if one is brave then recovery comes from within, through complete acceptance of suffering and death, and through the surrender of one's will and love of self."[v]

I fear, and do not pretend to understand, mental illness. I do not presume to prescribe for those who suffer from it. It is clear, though, that Van Gogh rejected the very thing he was so sure of: that acceptance, that surrender.

He knew that he had turned his back not only on health but life itself. "Yes, real life would be something else," he wrote, "but I don't think I belong to that category of souls who are ready to live, and also ready to suffer, at any moment."[vi]

Does anyone belong to such a category? Is it a question of categories? Is it not a question, finally, of what we want and how much we want it, who we want and how much we want him?

━

The thought of failure, of my failure to impress myself upon my fellows, tempts me to despair. It makes me suffer.

My despair, my pride, are one.

I will not know happiness till I forget myself. I will not have peace until my happiness becomes irrelevant.

~

I should like to accept, with cheer, my helplessness and God's mercy.

Is it possible to live in mercy? To wake to it, to accept it like the air I breathe?

~

I know what humility is not:

It is not balance, "the middle way," good choices.
It is not good nature, easy tolerance.
It is not a matter of style.
It is not dispirited: God's end is not to "put us in our
place."

~

*I*t is natural to make a list of prohibitions,[vii] but my real problem is what to *do:* how does one "live humbly with his God"? How does one live, each day, as one among others?

One has to start somewhere. So I begin my list:

Look, really look, at other people.
Ask. Tell if I need to tell, but learn to ask.
Listen to my fellows. Encourage them to talk about
themselves, and listen, for once, to what they say.
Tell the truth, and when the truth is that I don't
know, say it: "I don't know."
Take everyone as seriously as I take myself.

~

modest beginning. I do not expect much of myself. I have reason to distrust my lists, my resolutions.

I distrust myself.

～

Florence Allshorn, who founded St. Julian's, a Christian community of women in Sussex, was dismayed to find in her fellows, and in herself, "a really ghastly amount of self-centeredness."[viii] She was especially struck by "the misery caused by pride that refused to give in," and concluded, ruefully, that each invariably preferred that misery to humility.[ix] Allshorn observes that each member cherished a false picture of herself and endured, over time, the breaking of that picture.

Only the very young believe that community means harmony. We are born to pride, every one of us. Is it likely that we should be at peace with each other?

Humility begins with disillusionment, about ourselves, about those others who are like us. As to what happens next, it is not Step Five in the Manual of Christian Living. What happens next is prayer out of desperation.

Nothing more, really, than a cry.

～

God offers me a glimpse of myself, a glimpse that should leave me, except I remember God's mercy, in despair. I have honored no one; I did not honor my parents; I do not honor my wife or friends; I have cared for no one but myself. Should I not despair?

I understand the logic of despair.

What I do not understand is mercy. Why should God be merciful to me?

"I must start from where I am," declares Czesław Miłosz. "I am those monsters who visit my dreams / and reveal to me my hidden essence."[x]

"O wretched man that I am!" cries Paul.[xi]

My brothers.

Who can understand God's mercy?

⁓

Yes, I am tempted to despair.

Who, seeing clearly the world in which we live, seeing clearly himself, would not be tempted?

But I belong to our Lord. Who, knowing him, would not pray every day with all his heart against despair?

⁓

"I am not quite at the mercy of my own disquiet," I said.

Almost. Not quite.

I cannot like the thoughts that rise up from the dark within me.

"In every one of us," Miłosz insists, "a mad rabbit thrashes and a wolf pack howls, so that we are afraid it will be heard by others."[xii]

~

I want to learn, in the years I have left, compassion.

Compassion for my neighbors, who are as helpless as I. Compassion, perhaps, for myself.

~

I cannot, I know very well I cannot, survive on calculation, concealment; I can no longer pretend to myself, or to others, that I manage, direct, control what I have called my life.

I am not well: I say it.

Q. What then shall I do?

A. There is nothing I can do.

⁓

"*P*reserve me, O God," says the Psalmist, "for in you I put my trust."[xiii]

For.

There, right there: the note, unmistakable, of desperation. The Psalmist puts all his hope in one place *and in no place else:* if God does not preserve him, he is not preserved.

So it is with me. I too am desperate.

I too put all my trust in God.

⁓

hen Peter rebukes Jesus for what must seem to him an appalling defeatism, our Lord rebukes Peter in turn. Jesus commits himself to suffering; he will go to Jerusalem and be killed; he will endure it for the sake of others. "You are an offense to me," he tells his disciple; Peter minds the things of men, not the things of God.[xiv] "Deny yourself," our Lord goes on to say. "Take up your cross."[xv]

All this on the heels of a breakthrough: Jesus had asked his disciples directly, "But who do you say that I am?"[xvi] Peter's reply is dazzling, one of the glories of the Gospel: "You are the Christ, the Son of the living God."[xvii]

Peter knows, from this moment, that he cannot pretend to order, even to comprehend, his life. But if he knows it, he does not yet understand the implications of his loss, his gain. Like me, he does not yet know how to live.

In heaven, I believe, humility will mean "what is": the word will cease to have meaning. But here, on earth, it means obedience: to God, not to ambition or the spirit of the age. To the worldly, it must look like timidity, low spirits.

It is not timidity.

This must be my courage: to say no to myself.

"A servant is not greater than his master."[xviii]

~

Not a Virtue, but a Recognition

I cannot like my pride. I do not like to submit.

If I submit to pride, I submit to what Christians call The World, that cage of beasts who subjugate those weaker than themselves.

If I embrace humility, I submit myself to God, who loves me and commands me to love my neighbor.

Either way, I submit.

~

To ask is an act of humility. I do not like to ask. I do not like to admit my ignorance. I like even less to expose my need. I hide my need from those who love me: I have, I say with revealing, painful accuracy, my pride.

~

I have always been duplicitous. I wanted to devote myself entirely to God, but hoped, in my unfocused, huge ambition, to succeed in this world, too: to be respected, at the very least; to impress, if possible; to see my fellows in agreement with my pride.

Things have come to a point: I want God himself, I want him; I am willing to give up the rest.

Paul says it: "For you died, and your life is hidden with Christ in God."[xix] Jesus says it: "Deny yourself."

∿

*T*o abjure pride is, in fact, like dying. I fear the end of that familiar something I call I. I do not know, not really, what God means by it: what does he mean by dying?

My fear does not surprise me. What have I ever known but pride? I believe my Lord: I believe he will give me life. Nonetheless, I am afraid.

I don't know what it means to be alive.

∿

"If anyone desires to come after me, let him deny himself."

I do not know where this commandment ends. I do not know what will become of me.

I am willing to find out.

I do trust God, despite my fear.

I believe in him.

～

I am afraid.

What can I do? What can I do but pray?

This is my prayer: Lord, do your work in spite of me.

Do what you must.

～

Anxious. Praying is difficult; I can scarcely get the words out. I can't think, can't formulate sentences: "All's golden words are spent."

I pray.

God's mercy is not at the mercy of my eloquence. If all I can say is "Have mercy on me, Lord," he will hear me.

~

I am appalled, today, at my response to disappointment. A humble man should not fall so far. Nor should he be such easy prey to despair.

I learn nothing: I know nothing at all about humility. When anyone corrects me, I feel my pride surge up within me.

Put to the test, I defend myself with fury. My memory is a minefield of resentment and anger.

What can our Lord have to do with such a man? Why should he persist with me? The Psalmist is right: God will have to create in me a clean heart.[xx]

The one I have learns nothing; it does not change.

~

59

*L*ying awake: "the night watches." The truths I know will not cohere; what I know is confusion. One disheartening fact remains clear: for all God's love, for all his mercy, I cannot change my heart. How does such a one as I live with himself, with God? In continuous abasement? As though nothing were awry? "Seventy times seven," yes—but what is the fate of meaning itself when neither my heart, nor my actions, change?[xxi]

Though what I feel can scarcely be distinguished from hopelessness, I do have hope. I claim the fellowship of those who know despair and yet persist: the Psalmist crying "out of the depths";[xxii] John Donne, exasperated by his sin, doubting, for the moment, God's forgiveness, exclaiming, "When thou *has* done, thou hast not done, / For I have more";[xxiii] William Cowper, brought back from madness, concluding, "He is his own interpreter, / And he will make it plain."[xxiv]

⁓

I do not ask for "spiritual experiences"; I doubt they form the basis of any real faith. Nevertheless, I was, in the midst of prayer last night, overcome by a succession of reminders, every one from the Scriptures, every one delivered with such intensity, such warmth, such light—I admit I am groping for words—that I had no thought for myself at all:

And what does the Lord require of you but to do justly, to love mercy, and to walk humbly with your God? Come to me like a child. In returning and rest you shall be saved; in quietness and confidence shall be your strength. You are like a sheep with his shepherd, and under his watchful eye go in and out. Show mercy with cheerfulness. Pray without ceasing. I will give you rest.[xxv]

Each time God confronts me with myself and my delusions, each time I come to the end of my resources, each time I cry out in desperation, I arrive at the same relief, the same mercy in the end.

Despair is one of my temptations. I know enough to pray against despair.

I know my Lord will heal me. As surely as the woman who touched his robe, I know it.[xxvi]

This is what the Psalmist says: "The Lord takes pleasure in those who fear him, / In those who hope in his mercy."[xxvii]

I do hope in his mercy.

Not a Virtue, but a Recognition

At church, I gaze round at my fellows with something like envy. I think of myself, this morning, as a critical, cold spirit, a lover only of himself, a man who cannot escape himself, who has, on a whim, thrown in his lot with creatures from a warmer planet.

I am here on false pretenses, I tell myself: I am disqualified by my pride. My presence makes community, the very notion of Christ's body, impossible.

I do know, of course, that many of my fellows are as disinclined to fellowship as I, perhaps as thoroughly disaffected, and this knowledge, finally, reassures me. When I see the likes of us joined together, I must believe—I do believe—that Someone has joined us.

～

Someone has joined us.

～

Jesus tells his disciples, "It is the Father's good pleasure to give you the kingdom."[xxviii]

His will be done, then.

Confession

Lord, you have known me from afar.[i]

Regard me now, your lowly one.

~

My pride is ludicrous, absurd.

~

Have mercy, Lord.

"A Child in Tears for an Apple"

*H*ow little I understand!

I do not understand myself. What made me think I could understand myself?

I do not understand my God. Did I think to understand him?

I do not understand why he should move my heart.

~

"A Child in Tears for an Apple"

*H*ow little I understand!

What do I know, what do I really understand? I know I belong to God, that what delights me in my neighbors finds its origin in him. I am aware of my fragility. I know I cannot keep myself. I know I cannot keep myself alive.

I want to be at peace with God. To be at peace with what I cannot know. Not to yearn to be what I am not.

~

*A*m I the one who wills, or the one who is willed? The one who understands, or the understood?

When I began to pray for humility, I knew that it was *my* desire, my prayer. But it seems also to be true—I say this now, as I look back—that my desire was urged on me.

Why not? I know that God pursues us.

~

I don't understand my own will. How can I understand the will, the willing, of God?

I am too tired, too glad, to speculate further.

⁓

I feel, in fact, the weariness, the peace, of the convalescent. Have I come through?

Do I survive my pride?

My Lord, do what you will with me.

The fever of my life, the worst of it, is over: "The great rage, you see, is cur'd in him."[i]

Do not, I want to say to my friends, expect too much of me. I am ashamed. I am ashamed that pride, my pride, has so disrupted the lives of those who love me. How bitter it is to think about my selfishness, my outbursts of despair and anger!

I don't know what to do. I don't know what to do except to pray for mercy, for a heart of mercy toward others, for the will to love as I am loved.

I don't know if I'm happy. I don't know if it matters.

⁓

"A Child in Tears for an Apple"

$\mathcal{B}$ruised pride, I see now, sometimes passes for humility. But silence, deference, mask envy, contempt for others and ourselves.

Pride is pride. If we overcome our hurt, if we recover self-esteem, we find that we have little reason, after all, to esteem ourselves.

But we will come to mercy by and by.

~

$\mathcal{T}$hat one who is compelled to see himself, that one who is humbled by God, says Fénelon, knows very well that he is not what he thought he was—not wise, not in control, not the shoulderer of others' burdens: "Nor is he any longer self-satisfied, asking for nothing because he is too proud to ask. Nay, rather is he like a child in tears for an apple."[ii]

When one's pretty image of himself is shattered, he cannot continue as he was.

I am like a child in tears for an apple.

~

I do not hope for self-improvement. Perhaps I can improve my manners—I may have, in the course of my life, improved them—but I have not been able to improve my heart; I have not mellowed into wisdom. I am, in fact, every bit the fool I always was, as selfish, unreliable, impetuous and impatient as I was at twenty.

What can I say for myself?

Nothing, of course—and need not. I need not say a word to defend myself.

∽

My state is like despair, and not. I know despair: I have surrendered, in the past, to that temptation. So I know how to do this. I know how to count myself nothing.

This is the difference: desire. I want nothing *but:* I want nothing but my Lord himself. I give up what was dear to me, I give up everything I fought for, everything I claimed.

I am free to give up everything for him.

∽

As for my pride, what is it I renounce? Myself: that grand self I imagined, an illusion, something which does not exist.

I said no, I am saying no, to nothingness.

⌣

I want to be "like a tree beside the waters," to see those around me flourish, to have life and give life.[iii] I have met people, a few, around whom everyone seemed to be at ease, trusting, unafraid, free to be themselves, at peace. I want to be like them.

Is it permissible to ask for such a gift?

⌣

*I*n fact, I seldom listen to others; I almost never look, really look, at them. I glance, identify, move on.

When I think to listen, my reward is to be, more often than not, proved wrong. I am wrong about what and how my neighbors think, about what they feel. They surprise me. I can't finish their sentences.

I am not unhappy to be proved wrong.

I want to love God with all my heart, with all my soul, with all my mind, with all my strength.

As for my neighbors, perhaps the one love will inform the other.

～

*S*ometimes, for one brief startling moment, I see my friend as he was meant to be: no one but himself, at ease with me and with himself. For a moment, he is free from envy, wounded pride. A word, a gesture of kindness, of magnanimity, a beautiful lightness of spirit, and then he disappears again behind the fortifications of his pride.

Jesus will, "by the power of his resurrection," restore him, and this restoration is one of the reasons I look forward to heaven.[iv]

～

"A Child in Tears for an Apple"

How like we are, my friend and I. In him I see myself.

～

It has to be *our* father, as in the prayer our Lord taught his disciples. How could he be mine alone? Even I am not so proud as to think him mine alone.

I am one among others.

If I want to be loved by God, I must love my brothers and sisters.

I may not use, neglect, or sacrifice them for the sake of self-esteem.

No comparisons with others. No emulation.

～

*I*f God will make me one among others, if he will teach me to love my brothers and sisters, what can I say? They are his friends, and must be mine as well.

If he insist on changing my heart, what can I do?

As for me, what will become of me?

Is the question relevant?

⌒

I am ready to say it: "Thy will bee done, though in my owne undoing."ᵛ

⌒

"A Child in Tears for an Apple"

"The fear of the LORD is the beginning of wisdom."[vi]

"Walk humbly with your God."[vii]

With. Walk humbly *with your God*.

The God I have reason to fear does not intend me harm. Is it possible? He loves me.

He wants me to be with him.

～

I know what it means to say, "My God, my God." I know what it means to say, "You are my last, you were always my only hope."

I want more. I want to live in him, to be enlivened every day: in need, in fear, in relief, thanksgiving, praise; in exhaustion, in quiet; in sadness, in distraction; in dullness, in delight, to live in him.

～

I want humility because I want much more.

"*B*ehold the proud," says Habakkuk. "His soul is not upright in him; / But the just shall live by his faith."[viii]

Pride: a defect of the soul. Humility: to "live by faith," to believe in someone not ourselves. To live.

I want to live: I want to find out what it means to live.

When I said, "I feel the peace of the convalescent," I did not mean "I am cured."

I meant, instead, "I understand."

I understand, a little, my condition.

What I am, what I am not.

Who saves me.

⁓

No, I am not cured.

Some days, I am possessed. A spirit of irritability, of rebellion, possesses me.

This spirit—I have known it all my life—begins as dullness, indifference. The rebellion it engenders is rebellion in its purest form, without meaning, without cause.

I am surprised—and, I confess, relieved—to find this same appalling state of affairs in Herbert's *Temple*: "I struck the board and cry'd, No more. I will abroad."[ix] Herbert cannot, any more than I, explain himself; he is saved, exactly as I am saved, in spite of himself:

But as I rav'd and grew more fierce and wild
      At every word,
Me thoughts I heard one calling, *Child*:
      And I reply'd, *My Lord*.[x]

When I pray against this mood—if that is what it is—my Lord, our Lord, rescues me again.

∼

Last week, in the clutches of The Mood, I felt lifeless, without purpose; nothing in this world or the next possessed value. The sky, as intensely blue then as it is today, refused its color. Yet even then, God was alive.

My moods do not determine meaning.

∼

I may not trust myself.

Do I not, in fact, still yearn to know, to be the one who knows?

God gives me this much certainty, he makes me know this much: I do not understand myself. I cannot save myself.

⌒

*T*he trees along the street are bare now, waiting.

I think about my journal. Shall I keep it faithfully till spring? Shall I follow the familiar plot? Shall I anticipate, make use of spring, that giddy symbol of our hope?

No, winter is my season, now. It is my better symbol. It is the season, I believe, of all who see themselves, if only for a moment; all those who understand how desperate they are, they and their fellows.

Salvatore Quasimodo, in 1944, in occupied Milan, reviled the new grass, "the obscure sorcery of the earth," bursting up through the rubble of the ruined city.[xi] No, he declared, it would not suffice, this triumph of what we call the natural world. We cannot begin to live in hope, he asserted, without "a sign that reaches beyond life."[xii]

I have that sign that reaches beyond life, beyond this something we call life.

So I embrace it then, this bitter season by whose light I see my need.

I embrace it with hope.

I embrace it with thanksgiving.

~

My little journal, my record of defeat, of helplessness, must not be read, in the modern way, as a "cry for help." I need help, of course. But my history is by no means singular. My deficiencies, my fears, are those of every man and woman since the Fall.

~

"A Child in Tears for an Apple"

This is what I mean to say: I accept my weakness; I do not embrace it. I accept the weakness of my brothers and sisters. I pray for help, for hope. Hopelessness is my confession, not my creed.

~

There are men, I admit, and some women, who are so confident, so gifted, so lucky in their health and education, that they seem no less than gods. They accept their fortune gracefully, with scarcely, it seems to me, a thought. Many of them are kind. But it is hard for them to doubt themselves, to believe, against what seems such evidence, in their finiteness, their fallibility.

I do not envy them. I, who have unhappily discovered in myself a seam of envy, do not envy them.

How can one who is almost a god surrender himself? How can he say to God, "Your will, not mine, be done"?

~

There are Christians who admonish their fellows to "claim God's promises." I do not object, not really. But I cannot understand them.

Where will such a man as I, unable to control his own will, helpless against himself, pierced by the recognition of his pride, acquire such confidence?

Imagine such a man as I, shaking his fist at God and crying, "You said! You *said!*"

I do, of course, cry out to God; I do—I confess it—rail, cajole, accuse. But I understand, God understands, I cry out as a child cries out.

I do not make claims.

What does humility look like?

Here is a child, our Lord says: look at him.[xiii]

He understands, this child, that he is vulnerable. A lost child is afraid and right to be afraid.

He knows he cannot save himself.

*I*s it possible? Sometimes, now, I listen to my fellows with pleasure. I like the sound of their voices, their verbal quirks, their gestures, the way they think. I like the fact that I don't really understand them. I like their *other*ness.

When I visit my friend, who is ill and short of breath, she says, "You talk." Is it possible? I can't think how to talk to her without questions. I! I who have always talked and never listened.

For most of my more than fifty years, I have listened to no one but myself.

~

I allow my fellows to help me.

I cannot refuse them. There is no denying that I need their help.

Can I refuse their generosity, their hope, their consolation, their good cheer?

Who am I to refuse them?

~

I have never in my life been proved so wrong, so often, about so many things.

How hard it is, and how good, to be proved wrong!

To live in pride is to live closed off from, to live unaware of, the richness of God.

When I spend the morning at my neighbor's house, waiting to admit the city inspector, I poke through the books on her shelves and look, really look, at the pictures on her walls.

Why this book, I wonder. Why this one? Why Dubuffet? Why George Macdonald?[xiv]

Who is this woman I have "known" for twenty-five years?

I realize how slightly I know even my friends, how pride has kept me from knowing anyone. How sudden and how deep, my sorrow, my regret!

I dishonor my friend. By my inattention, I dishonor her.

～

"A Child in Tears for an Apple"

Shall I live by sorrow, by regret?

What does humility look like? I resolve to ask, "Why do you love these books, these pictures?"

Tell me who you are.

Perhaps I am ready, now, to listen.

~

My faith is meager, I am easily distracted. I forget, for most of a day, to pray.

Do I forget my Lord?

It is worse than I imagined. What to do, when I can scarcely bring myself to pray?

I begin. I make myself begin.

I am so destitute, I ask God, in the midst of prayer, to give me words and will to pray.

~

/ have been warned. My older friends assure me that at sixty I will "become invisible."

Let it be so!

I pray against my pride. I begin to pray for my neighbors.

I mean to pull my cloak about me, this cloak of invisibility which both protects and blesses me, and watch my neighbors, and my God, without distraction.[xv]

⌒

What does this mean: "I have come that they may have life, and that they may have it more abundantly"?[xvi] What does Jesus mean when he says of the one who believes in him, "Out of his heart will flow rivers of living water"?[xvii]

What does he mean?

⌒

"A Child in Tears for an Apple"

For me, "how to live" must come down, finally, to small, particular, impossible things.

How do I accept my friend's success without envy?

How do I accept his weakness, his defeat, without smugness and secret pleasure?

How do I drive my car without anger?

How, in a sudden gust of understanding, do I recognize my pride and not despair?

∼

I suspect my anger at myself. Why should I be angry at myself? My frustration springs from self-love, "which is troubled and disquieted to see itself imperfect."[xviii]

Is there no end of pride?

∼

Sometimes I am angry at myself for being angry. Shall I keep on, angry because I am angry at myself for being angry?

At this point, I laugh at myself, relieved to find myself a fool. Pride is, surely, though I can seldom laugh at myself, a laughing matter.

That God crush my pride is not the point.

That I deny myself is not the point.

The point is that my ears be opened and I hear God say, "Look child: look what I have for you."

"A Child in Tears for an Apple"

My Lord, my Lord. I want life. I desire, I lack, that very thing you wish to give to me.

～

Like Orlando in Shakespeare's *As You Like It*, tired of play-acting, missing his Rosalind, I can "no longer live by thinking."[xix] I want nothing but my Lord himself. I don't want to theorize. I don't want to talk about him. I want him.

I surrender what I must surrender, suffer what I must. Without my Lord, what am I?

I am not myself apart from him.

～

I should like to sit in a room with others and not say a word.

I should like to listen to others talking and not feel the need to "have my say."

I should like to be happy in the happiness of others.

I should like to accept, with cheerfulness, their help, their cheer.

I should like to feel delight, every time, at the prospect of prayer.

⁓

I say it more with wonderment than sadness: everyone I know is kinder, more observant, more compassionate, more generous than I.

How could I not have noticed?

I have always begrudged my time. I feel no compulsion to "minister to others." If I care now for anyone besides myself, what can I say? None of this is my doing.

Perhaps I am given, the way a bride is given, allows herself to be given, by her father.

⁓

"A Child in Tears for an Apple"

To watch over, without seeming to watch over; to allow oneself to be watched over.

To do, or not do, as love prompts.

Not to reject oneself; in fact, to find a place there to begin: "And just as you want men to do to you, you also do to them likewise."[xx]

~

God blesses him, that man whose pride is crushed, who has been defeated. He rewards him for nothing.

"He hardly recognizes himself," says André Louf.[xxi]

Such a man has nothing, knows he has nothing, can do nothing but give thanks. He marvels at God, who gives him what he needs and more, more than he could ever have imagined.

~

hardly recognize myself.

⌣

My Lord, you know the ache I cannot put into words, the love I do not know how to express. I do not know my heart so well as you know it.

Today you give me gifts I do not know how to describe. I did not ask for them. I did not know to ask.

How shall I praise you, Lord? I have no words.

⌣

"A Child in Tears for an Apple"

Lord, have mercy on me and everyone, and every creature, I have offended. Lord, have mercy on everyone and every creature who has been offended, by me or any one of us.

My Lord, let me see them all in heaven, healed. Let me kneel before them.

~

My Lord Jesus, just to hear you speak is health to me. To hear you speak at all, to hear your voice.

My Lord, the very sound of your voice is health to me.

~

Lord, what I thought my own was always yours. I had no reason to be proud.

I accept your gifts, I accept them all.

Do I begin to understand you? I understand this much: you are the One Who Gives.

Give me, then, that heart which says, "I need nothing, I want nothing, Lord, but you."

Take what you will, Lord.

I am not afraid.

⁓

Am I not dispensed? My very helplessness dispenses me to ask God what I please.

If I ask badly, out of ignorance, will God cease to be God? Is he not the God of mercy?

⁓

I am tired of thinking, tired of words. I want to be quiet.

And I need not speak. I see now that I need not formulate, defend, maintain myself. When I fall silent, I remain myself.

God, meanwhile, remains God. He remains himself.

I need not fear for him or for myself.

~

*W*hen we "walk humbly with our God," we will, I think, be free. But my question remains: how will we live? What will we be freed to do? Will we not laugh, sleep, eat, drink, work, and play? Will not our Lord, pretending not to watch, watch over us?

Like those sheep in John's Gospel, will we not be more than merely safe?[xxii] We will cheerfully "go in and out." We will be ourselves and no more than ourselves. We will be free: happy at last, without knowing what happiness means.

~

How can one see one's pride, see that he lives by it and in it?

How does a fish learn that his element is water?

By being drawn up, forcibly taken, to lie gasping and flopping in unfamiliar air.

I am attempting to live now in such unfamiliar air. The atmosphere of the kingdom of heaven will, I am certain, be the death of me.

And give me life, I am told. I begin to believe it.

6

WORKING IT OUT

Long before the cold, the darkness arrived, I called these hopes and hesitations, these desperate cries, my Winter Journal. Now that winter is here, I embrace it, this season of want, this ancient symbol of negation.

God lays bare my disastrous heart; he exposes my every illusion. What I claimed for myself, he has taken away.

I am not unhappy. It is good to know the truth about myself. It is good to be so certain of God's mercy.

I am each day bemused at the nearness, the attentiveness of God.

Why should he attend me?

When he shows nothing of himself, when he seems not to attend me, I am not afraid. He may do as he pleases.

He is God. I am his creature.

Working It Out

I think less often, now, about myself.

I have few words. Sometimes, in prayer, I manage nothing more than thanks. It is enough.

~

Sometimes, now, I wake to a new emotion, new at least to me. I think of it as a kind of fear. I believe it to be wonder.

I don't know what will happen. I do not know how to prepare myself.

Can one prepare oneself?

~

*I*t is enough, I think, to live in mercy and accept what—who—God brings.

⁓

I am free to look at my fellows.

How beautiful they are!

It is possible to contemplate my fellows.

I began Haruki Murakami's *Norwegian Wood* last evening and read late into the night. When I fell asleep, its intonation took control of my dreams. I woke this morning under the influence, still, of Murakami's beautiful privation, his almost weightless despair. How fragile we are, I kept thinking. How helpless we are!

Everyone alive keeps breaking my heart.

⁓

Working It Out

J　How beautiful they are!

How little I know them, my neighbors.

How little I know them!

～

J　Be a servant, Jesus says.[i]

What does a servant do, but wait?

Sometimes now I stop, I stop thinking, I wait for my fellows, I wait on them because I do not understand them. In conversation I wait, I do not interrupt.

"Study to be quiet," says Paul.[ii]

Don't talk. Don't presume.

～

I do not miss my old positions of authority. I do not miss my old compulsions, my consuming pleasures.

I no longer miss our old house—surely a house, for what remains of my life, will be a house and no more than a house.

Though these things seemed everything to me, I do not miss them.

~

I approach this season of short days, long nights, with apprehension, gladness; with fear and trembling, with expectation.

~

I will not survive this winter unscathed.

～

"*Work* out your own salvation," Paul advises, "with fear and trembling."[iii]

I begin to understand him.

How can Paul tell us what today will bring? Jesus is alive; he has spoken, he has spoken to Paul. What Paul knows now, he knows absolutely; everything else is cast into uncertainty. Anything might happen, and he knows it.

How to live: quietly, alertly, in hope despite appearances, in expectation, in fear and trembling.

Each day working it out.

～

*F*ear and trembling.

Could it be otherwise?

Like Abraham, I "do not know where I am going."[iv]

I do not know.

"Now I am here," complains George Herbert, "what thou wilt do with me / None of my books will show."[v]

～

*O*ne can hear from this house in the city the muted roar, the steady faint susurrus, of traffic on the nearby interstate highway. Sometimes I am quiet enough, aware enough, to hear it, this lovely sound which puts me so in mind of the Spirit. It seems a beckoning, an invitation.

Am I ready to move on?

Tonight I listen. I lie awake, both happy and afraid, attentive.

～

"Watch and pray."[vi]

One among others, under the mercy of our Lord, I watch.

⁓

At Gethsemene, Jesus woke his disciples and asked, "What? Could you not watch with me one hour?"[vii]

With. That beautiful word, like *our* and *us* in the prayer he taught us.

"Inasmuch as you did it to one of the least of these my brethren, you did it to me," he says, and I infer that "the body of Christ" is more a body than I knew.[viii]

When I watch with my brothers and sisters—for love, for comfort, on guard against the Tempter, for our Lord's return—I watch with him.

⁓

*H*ome from college, my former students meet me for coffee, to reminisce, to regale me with stories. Everything is new to them—everything, however difficult or painful, excites them, moves them. I accept the gift of their adventures.

As for me, I look ahead, when I allow myself to look ahead, with trepidation and with wonder.

I said that I would not survive this winter unscathed. Let it be so! I no longer wish to "make my mark."

I want God to leave his mark on me.

⁓

*I*f my heart is better, it is not healed. I am not charitable; I give no one his due, her due. I am a boorish listener, presumptuous, disrespectful.

This is the one to whom God is so merciful, the one he showers with blessings.

⁓

*D*o I progress? As I look back through the pages of my Winter Journal, I see my "progress" well enough: one day I surprise myself with what seems, at least, a new spirit; the next I see my pride at work, still virulent, still resistant.

Progress isn't, at any rate, the right word. The truth is that I have given up; with relief I give up all my hopes.

I am living, I know it, by the grace of God.

⌒

*W*hen I asked for humility, I did not know what I was asking. I could not have known. I could not foresee that God would take so little, give so much.

Today I sit in my neighbors' kitchen, with a child—not my child—on one knee and the big curly head of a dog—not my dog—against the other. I am safe here; these are my brothers and sisters. I may be quiet.

"Assuredly I say to you," declares Jesus, "there is no one who has left house or brothers or sisters or father or mother or wife or children or lands for my sake and the gospel's, who shall not receive a hundredfold now in this time—houses and brothers and sisters and mothers and children and lands."[ix]

I know that he does not mean "you will have what those who love themselves want always—things to set them above their neighbors, things to affirm their own pre-eminence." And I know very well that he adds, "with persecutions."

I say little for myself. I have suffered only what a proud man, ready to be taught humility, must suffer. But I begin to understand my Lord.

When I said to God, "Take what you will," I discovered a secret. What is this secret? Simply that God gives. He is the One Who Gives.

To Give is the principle of heaven: "Give and it will be given to you: good measure, pressed down, shaken together, and running over."[x]

⁓

Like a young prince, I stretch out my arms. Every house is my house, every child my child.

As for persecutions, what can I do? What can I do but accept them?

I am not my own.

"A servant is not greater than his master."

⁓

Do I come to the end of knowledge? I understand what I am given to understand.

It is enough.

It is more than enough.

⁓

I am not certain I could bear more knowledge, or more joy, than I am given. "How little of the sea," exclaims Samuel Rutherford, "can a child carry in his hand!"[xi]

I am not certain that my body has strength enough to bear this life I am given, this expectation, this nearness of joy, the fearsome, beautiful incomprehensibility of God.

Is this, then, what it means to be alive? To be at that point, always, where my knowledge ends?

⁓

Look at him: here is a man surviving what should be, for him, a dark season. One thing after another is taken from him. He knows, this man, what it means to be defeated.

But he gives thanks for his defeats. His heart overflows.

He is—he knows it—merely one among others.

He is one of them.

⌣

I am dispensed. I am dispensed from disappointment, from resentment. My time was never my time, my life never—how silly I was!—my own.

There is no explaining what has happened to me. I do not try to explain it.

Whatever awaits me, I know this to be true: I am a man more blessed than he deserves.

⌣

I have lost control of my life.

Do not fear for me: I say it, after all, with laughter, with relief.

I say it with lightness of heart.

⁓

I do not reject myself. I do not denigrate myself.

No, I forget myself. I am permitted, I am safe enough, to forget myself.

⁓

*T*his is what I know, so far, about humility, about that man who is humbled:

He does the work God sets before him; the work itself scarcely matters.

He wants nothing; he wants nothing but God himself. He knows there is no meaning at all outside of God.

Knowing his incapacity, he understands the failings of others. He knows that neither they nor he can help themselves. He lives, he knows he lives every day, by the mercy of God.

"In his presence," he exclaims, "is fullness of joy."[xii]

He is like a man who has died, who comes back to his old haunts for a time and looks about, bemused. Nothing matters to him but the will, the good pleasure of his Lord.

*A*ll right, I can say it now: to be loved is better than to be admired.

Working It Out

As for the tasks God puts before me, any fool could do them. In the past, when I wanted what was worthy of me, work commensurate with my abilities, my "gifts," I might have spurned them.

One task is the same as another, now.

What matters is the one who lays it before me.

~

I have no power to change my heart, my recalcitrant heart. I cannot change my heart.

I throw up my hands and watch God do what he will do.

How fierce, how loving, is my God, who against his better judgment, loves me: "Mercy and truth have met together; righteousness and peace have kissed."[xiii]

~

When admiration for others rises in me, when I praise against my will, I am made free. I am freed from self.

In defiance of my pride, I offer praise.

When I praise another, my heart is light. When I praise God, I live, for the nonce, in heaven.

"Praise," says the Psalmist, "is beautiful."[xiv]

∽

Jesus, walking on the Sea of Galilee, calls to his terrified disciples, "It is I; do not be afraid."[xv]

Just so. One is afraid, then not afraid.

When he who kills and brings to life,[xvi] who "speaks and it is done," says not to be afraid, I am not afraid.[xvii]

I go on, I dare go on, in this season of negation I go on, afraid and not afraid.

∽

"Surely I have calmed and quieted my soul," says the Psalmist. "Like a weaned child with his mother ; / Like a weaned child is my soul within me."[xviii]

~

Did I call it "my life"?

I give over such distinctions.

I do call it, I dare call it life.

I feel the stirrings of life within me.

NOTES

Chapter 1. Something Has Happened

i.   *Let my change come:* See Job 14.14, KJV. "If a man die, shall he live again? all the days of my appointed time will I wait, till my change come."

Chapter 2. A Prayer Against Myself

i.   *"The secret things belong to the Lord our God":* Deut. 29.29.

ii. *"a stone, a plant, a microbe":* Jean-Paul Sartre, *Nausea,* 116.

iii. *I was blind:* cf. Blaise Pascal, *Pensées,* 19. "There is no reason for me to be here rather than there, now rather than then. Who put me here? By whose command and act were this time and place allotted to me?"

iv. *"This poor man cried":* Ps. 34.6., KJV.

v.   *I am the man who, in conversation:* Bernard, Abbot of Clairvaux, *The Steps of Humility,* 13.41.

vi. *"I am not as other men are":* ibid., 13.42.

vii. *Proust is right:* Marcel Proust, *Within a Budding Grove,* 573.

viii. *"By the word of the Lord":* Ps. 33.6, 9.

ix. *"It is good for me":* Ps. 119.71.

x.   *"Let us make a name for ourselves":* Gen. 11.4.

xi. *"Those who do not gather with me":* Matt. 12.30.

xii. *"How often I wanted":* Matt. 23.37.

xiii. *"Assuredly, I say to you":* Matt. 19.23-26. See also Mark 10.23-27.

xiv. *"Richard loves Richard":* William Shakespeare, *Richard III,* 5.3.184.

xv. *"He has scattered the proud":* Luke 1.51.

xvi. *"Disassembled man":* Derek Walcott, *The Prodigal,* 53.

Chapter 3. Pitiful Fledgling

i.   *"I never knew you":* Matt. 7.23.

ii. *"unaccommodated man":* William Shakespeare, *King Lear,* 3.4.104-105. "Thou art the thing itself," Lear tells the ragged, apparently witless Edgar: "Unaccommodated man is no more but such a poor, bare, forked animal as thou art."

iii. *"with charity instead of partiality":* C. S. Lewis, "Two Ways with the Self," *God in the Dock: Essays on Theology and Ethics,* 194.

iv. *blessed, unaware:* The allusion is to Samuel Taylor Coleridge, "The Rime of the Ancient Mariner," *Poems of Samuel Taylor Coleridge,* 186-209, lines 282-287. The mariner's sudden change of heart about the water-snakes, the "thousand slimy things" that swarm round the vessel, marks the turning point of the poem:

> O happy living things! no tongue
> Their beauty might declare:
> A spring of love gushed from my heart,
> And I blessed them unaware:
> Sure my kind saint took pity on me,
> And I blessed them unaware.

v.   *"Do not let your left hand know":* Matt. 6.3.

vi.   *"enjoys the air it breathes":* William Wordsworth, "Lines Written in Early Spring," *The Poetical Works of Wordsworth,* 81-82, lines 11-12.

vii.   *"For whoever exalts himself":* Luke 14.11, 18.14; Matt. 23.12.

viii.   *"one man loved the pilgrim soul in you":* W. B. Yeats, "When You Are Old," *Collected Poems of W. B. Yeats,* 40-41, lines 7-8. Gonne, for years the object of Yeats's devotion, and often his verse, married Major John MacBride, instead of the poet, in 1903.

ix.   *"I greet him the days I meet him":* Gerard Manley Hopkins, "The Wreck of the *Deutschland,"* *The Poems of Gerard Manley Hopkins,* 51-63, line 40.

x.   *"too high for me":* Ps. 131.1, KJV.

xi.   *"Take my yoke upon you":* Matt. 11.29.

xii.   *"Master, it is good for us":* Luke 9.33.

xiii.   *"What is man, that you are mindful of him":* Ps. 8.4.

xiv.   *"What is man, that you should exalt him:* Job 7.17.

xv. *"I have uttered"*: Job 42.3.

xvi. *At my conversion:* cf. Abraham Heschel, *Man Is Not Alone,* 93. "Faith precedes any palpable experience, rather than derives from it."

Chapter 4. Not A Virtue, but a Recognition

i. *"done what was your duty to do"*: Luke 17.10.

ii. *"how to stay quietly in my room"*: Pascal, *Pensées,* 37. "Sometimes, when I set to thinking about the various activities of men, the dangers and troubles which they face at Court, or in war, giving rise to so many quarrels and passions, daring and often wicked enterprises and so on, I have often said that the sole cause of man's unhappiness is that he does not know how to stay quietly in his room."

iii. *"Come to me"*: Matt. 11.28.

iv. *"I trust in the mercy"*: Ps. 52.8.

v. *"I'm sure that if one is brave"*: Vincent Van Gogh to Theo Van Gogh, 7 or 8 September 1889, *Letters of Vincent Van Gogh,* 464.

vi. *"Yes, real life"*: ibid, 464.

vii. *It is natural to make a list:* See, for example, Jonathan Edwards, *Charity and its Fruits,* vol. 8, 239-243.

viii. *"a really ghastly amount"*: Florence Allshorn, "The St. Julian's Community," in J. H. Oldham, *Florence Allshorn and the Story of St. Julian's,* 83.

ix. *"the misery caused by pride"*: ibid., 87.

x. *"I must start":* Czesław Miłosz, "To Raja Rao," *New and Collected Poems, 1931-2003,* 254-256, lines 40-42.

xi. *"O wretched man that I am":* Rom. 7.24.

xii. *"In every one of us":* Czesław Miłosz, "Report," *New and Collected Poems, 1931-2003,* 589-590, line 8.

xiii. *"Preserve me, O God":* Ps. 16.1.

xiv. *"You are an offense to me":* Matt. 16.22-23.

xv. *"Deny yourself":* Matt. 16.24. "Then Jesus said to his disciples, 'If anyone desires to come after Me, let him deny himself, and take up his cross, and follow Me.'"

xvi. *"But who do you say that I am?":* Matt. 16.15.

xvii. *"You are the Christ":* Matt. 16.16.

xviii. *"A servant is not greater than his master":* John 13.16, 15.20.

xix. *"For you died":* Col. 3.3.

xx. *The Psalmist is right:* Ps. 51.10. "Create in me a clean heart, O God, / and renew a steadfast spirit within me."

xxi. *"Seventy times seven":* Matt. 18.21-22. "Then Peter came to Him and said, 'Lord, how often shall my brother sin against me, and I forgive him? Up to seven times?' Jesus said to him, 'I do not say to you, up to seven times, but up to seventy times seven.'"

xxii. *The Psalmist crying:* Ps. 130.1.

xxiii. *"When thou hast done":* John Donne, "A Hymne to God the Father," *The Complete English Poems,* 490-491, lines 5, 11, 17.

xxiv. *William Cowper concluding:* William Cowper, "Light Shining Out of Darkness," *Poetical Works of William Cowper,* 485, lines 23-24.

xxv. *"And what does the Lord require of you . . . I will give you rest":* Mic. 6.8, Isa. 30.15, John 10.9, Rom. 12.8, 1 Thess. 5.17, Matt. 11.28.

xxvi. *As surely as the woman:* Matt. 9.20-22.

xxvii. *"The Lord takes pleasure":* Ps. 147.11.

xxviii. *"It is the Father's good pleasure":* Luke 12.32.

Confession

i. *Lord, you have known me:* Ps. 138.6. "Though the Lord is on high, yet he regards the lowly; / But the proud he knows from afar."

Chapter 5. "A Child in Tears for an Apple"

i. *"The great rage, you see":* Shakespeare, *King Lear,* 4.7.77-78.

ii. *"Nor is he any longer self-satisfied":* Fénelon to Madame la Comtesse de Montberon, n.d., *Letters of Love and Counsel,* 238.

iii. *"like a tree beside the waters":* Ps. 1.3.

iv. *"by the power of his resurrection":* Phil. 3.10.

v.   "*Thy will bee done*": Sir Thomas Browne, *Religio Medici,* in *"Religio Medici"and Other Works,* ed. L. C. Martin, 75.

vi.   "*The fear of the LORD is the beginning of wisdom*": Ps. 111.10, Prov. 9.10.

vii.   "*Walk humbly with your God*": Mic. 6.8.

viii. "*Behold the proud*": Hab. 2.4.

ix.   "*I struck the board and cry'd*": George Herbert, "The Collar," *Complete English Works,* 149-150, lines 1-2.

x.   *But as I raved:* ibid., lines 33-36.

xi.   "*the obscure sorcery of the earth*": Salvatore Quasimodo, "19 Gennaio 1944," *Tutte le poesie,* 230-231, line 17. The translation is mine.

xii.   "*a sign that reaches beyond life*": ibid, line 16. The concluding lines of Quasimodo's poem are striking:

> We seek a sign that reaches beyond life,
> Beyond the obscure sorcery of the earth
> Where even now, through tombs of rubble,
> The grass, malignant, urges up its flower.

xiii. *Here is a child, our Lord says:* Matt. 18.2-3. "Then Jesus called a little child to Him, and set him in the midst of them, and said, 'Assuredly I say to you, unless you are converted and become as little children, you will by no means enter the kingdom of heaven.'"

xiv.   *Why Dubuffet? Why George Macdonald?:* Jean Dubuffet (1901-1985), born in Le Havre, was a painter, sculptor, and graphic artist. The Scotsman

George Macdonald (1824-1905) is the author of *Lilith, Phantastes,* and several children's classics, including *The Princess and the Goblin* and *At the Back of the North Wind.*

xv. *I mean to pull my cloak about me:* With apologies to J. K. Rowling, whose Harry Potter possesses just such a cape.

xvi. *"I have come that they may have life":* Jn. 10.10.

xvii. *"Out of his heart will flow":* Jn. 7.38.

xviii. *self-love, "which is troubled and disquieted"*: St. Francis de Sales, *Introduction to a Devout Life,* 167. "Besides, this anger and vexation against ourselves tend to pride, and flow from no other source than self-love, which is troubled and disquieted to see itself imperfect."

xix. *I can "no longer live by thinking":* William Shakespeare, *As You Like It,* 5.2.50.

xx. *"And just as you want men to do":* Luke 6.31. See also Matt. 7.12.

xxi. *"He hardly recognizes himself":* André Louf, *The Way of Humility,* 21. "Such a person has henceforward attained a profound peace because his whole being has been destroyed and rebuilt by grace. He hardly recognizes himself. He has become a different person."

xxii. *Like those sheep in John's Gospel:* Jn. 10.9. "I am the door. If anyone enters by Me, he will be saved, and will go in and out and find pasture."

Chapter 6. Working It Out

i. *Be a servant, Jesus says:* Matt. 20.27-28. "And who-
    ever desires to be first among you, let him be your
    slave—just as the Son of Man did not come to be
    served, but to serve."

ii. *"Study to be quiet":* I Thess. 4.11, KJV.

iii. *"Work out your own salvation":* Phil. 2.12.

iv. *Like Abraham:* Heb. 11.8.

v. *"Now I am here":* George Herbert, "Affliction I,"
    Complete English Works, 44-46, lines 55-56.

vi. *"Watch and pray":* Matt. 26.41, Mark 14.38.

vii. *"What? Could you not watch":* Matt. 26.40.

viii. *"Inasmuch as you did it":* Matt. 25.40.

ix. *"Assuredly I say to you":* Mark 10.29-30.

x. *"Give and it will be given to you":* Luke 6.38.

xi. *"How little of the sea":* Samuel Rutherford, to Mat-
    thew Mowat, 1637, *Letters of Samuel Rutherford,*
    189.

xii. *"In his presence":* Ps. 16.11.

xiii. *"Mercy and truth have met together":* Ps. 85.10.

xiv. *"Praise," says the Psalmist, "is beautiful":* Ps. 147.1.

xv. *"It is I; do not be afraid":* Matt. 14.27.

xvi. *When he who kills and brings to life:* Deut. 32.39.
    "Now see that I, even I, am He, / And there is no
    God besides me; / I kill and I make alive; / I wound

and I heal; / Nor is there any who can deliver from my hand."

xvii. *who "speaks and it is done":* Ps. 33.9.

xviii. *"Surely I have calmed and quieted my soul":* Ps. 131. 2.

BIBLIOGRAPHY

Allshorn, Florence. "The St. Julian's Community." Oldham, J. H. *Florence Allshorn and the Story of St. Julian's.* New York: Harper & Brothers, n.d. 75-112.

Bernard, Abbot of Clairvaux. *The Steps of Humility.* Trans. George Bosworth Burch. Cambridge, MA: Harvard University Press, 1940.

Browne, Sir Thomas. *Religio Medici.* In *"Religio Medici" and Other Works.* Ed. L. C. Martin. Oxford: Clarendon Press, 1964. 1-80.

Coleridge, Samuel Taylor. *The Poems of Samuel Taylor Coleridge.* Ed. Ernest Hartley Coleridge. London: Oxford University Press, 1949.

Cowper, William. *The Poetical Works of William Cowper.* Ed. H. S. Milford. 4th ed. London: Oxford University Press, 1950.

De Sales, Francis, Saint. *Introduction to a Devout Life.* Ed. and Trans. Thomas Kepler. Cleveland: World, 1952.

Donne, John. *The Complete English Poems.* Ed. C. A. Patrides. New York: Alfred A. Knopf, 1991.

Fénelon [François de Selignac de la Mothe]. *Letters of Love and Counsel.* Trans. John McEwen. New York: Harcourt, Brace & World, 1964.

Herbert, George. *The Complete English Works.* Ed. Ann Pasternak Slater. New York: Alfred A. Knopf, 1995.

Heschel, Abraham. *Man Is Not Alone: A Philosophy of Religion.* New York: Farrar, Straus & Young, 1951.

Holy Bible. New King James Version. All Biblical quotations are from the New King James Version unless otherwise noted.

Hopkins, Gerard Manley. *The Poems of Gerard Manley Hopkins.* Ed. W. H. Gardner and N. H. MacKenzie. 4th ed. London: Oxford University Press, 1967.

Lewis, C. S. "Two Ways with the Self." *God in the Dock: Essays on Theology and Ethics.* Ed. Walter Hooper. Grand Rapids, MI: William B. Eerdmans, 1970. 193-195.

Louf, André. *The Way of Humility.* Kalamazoo, MI: Cistercian Publishers, 2007.

Miłosz, Czesław. *New and Collected Poems, 1931-2001.* New York: Ecco, 2003.

Murakami, Haruki. *Norwegian Wood.* Trans. Jay Rubin. New York: Vintage International, 2000.

Pascal, Blaise. *Pensées.* Trans. A. J. Krailsheimer. London: Penguin, 1995.

Proust, Marcel. *Within a Budding Grove.* Trans. C. K. Scott Moncrieff and Terence Kilmartin. Rev. D. J. Enright. New York: Modern Library, 1992.

Quasimodo, Salvatore. *Tutte le poesie.* Milan: Arnoldo Mondadori, 1960.

Rutherford, Samuel. *The Letters of Samuel Rutherford.* Ed. Frank E. Gaebelein. Chicago: Moody Press, 1951.

Sartre, Jean-Paul. *Nausea.* Trans. Lloyd Alexander. London: Hamish Hamilton, 1962.

Shakespeare, William. *As You Like It*. Ed. S. C. Burchell. Yale Shakespeare. New Haven and London: Yale University Press, 1965.

—. *The Tragedy of King Lear*. Ed. Tucker Brooke and William Lyon Phelps. Yale Shakespeare. New Haven and London: Yale University Press, 1963.

—. *The Tragedy of Richard III*. Ed. Jack R. Crawford. Yale Shakespeare. New Haven and London: Yale University Press, 1965.

Van Gogh, Vincent. *The Letters of Vincent Van Gogh*. Ed. Ronald de Leeuw. Trans. Arnold Pomerans. London: Allen Lane, 1996.

Walcott, Derek. *The Prodigal*. New York: Farrar, Straus & Giroux, 2004.

Wordsworth, William. *The Poetical Works of Wordsworth*. Ed. Paul Sheets. Boston: Houghton, Mifflin, 1982.

Yeats, W. B. *The Poems*. Ed. Richard J. Finneran. Vol 1 of *The Collected Works of W. B. Yeats*. 14 vols. New York: Macmillan, 1989.

About
Bruce Ray Smith

*B*ruce Ray Smith was born in Dunedin, Florida, in 1952. He spent most of his life as a teacher, and eventually acquired a Ph.D in English literature, from Washington University in St. Louis. Though unquestionably a Christian living in, and struggling with, the twenty-first century, his love of seventeenth-century English prose is evident in *Winter Light*, his first book.

The part of his life most relevant to *Winter Light* began in 1980, when he returned from L'Abri Fellowship in Greatham, England (he was a student, not a teacher), to join a small group of Christians who had moved to,and formed a church in, a poor, racially mixed neighborhood on the north side of St. Louis. Most of them, who were young then, are still in the same neighborhood thirty years later, and remain a tight-knit community. Bruce chose not to pursue an academic career when he realized that the meaning of his life was tied, in every way, to his church (Grace and Peace Church) and his neighborhood.

For more information about Bruce, visit the website www.bruceraysmith.com.

ABOUT KALOS PRESS

Kalos Press was established to give a voice to literary fiction, memoir, devotional writing, and Christian Reflection, of excellent quality, outside of the mainstream Christian publishing industry.

We believe that good writing is beautiful in form and in function, and is capable of being an instrument of transformation. It is our hope and ambition that every title produced by Kalos Press will live up to this belief.

For more information about Kalos Press, *Winter Light*, and/or other titles, or for ordering information, visit us on our website: www.kalospress.org, or contact us by e-mail at info@kalospress.org.

KIND WORDS ABOUT
WINTER LIGHT

*I*n the honest pages of *Winter Light*, I found the prideful secrets of my own heart revealed. As I read I breathed a quiet, "me too." Bruce Ray Smith's particular quest for humility gives voice to our common longing for transformation. We want to be changed, but the heart is deceitful above all things. We want to know God in our very bones, but there is a cost. With poetic and personal style, Smith offers a deeply insightful reflection on pride and humility that flows from the narrative of his life and prayers. *Winter Light* is that rare kind of book, where literary writing meets lived, biblical theology. It's a treasure!

Andi Ashworth
Author, Co-Director of Art House America
Nashville, TN

~

I commend Bruce Ray Smith's book *Winter Light*. Once I had begun to read I could not stop—both because of the raw power of the content and because of the brevity and starkness of the style which match the subject so well. I was deeply moved by its sometimes painful honesty and by the moments of profound joy that light up these pages.

Bruce is acutely insightful in his analysis of our arrogant and self-centered manner of living and of our need to recognize our spiritual poverty and to discover our dependence on the support and love of others. This slim volume deserves to be widely and often read. I know that I will return to it again and again and use it as an aid for my own self-reflection and prayers. The endless patience and grace of God shines a bright light across this bleak landscape of the heart.

Jerram Barrs
Professor of Christianity and Contemporary Culture
Resident Scholar at the Francis Schaeffer Institute
Covenant Theological Seminary
St. Louis, Missouri

⌒

When Martin Luther penned the first of The Ninety-five Theses, "When our Lord and Master, Jesus Christ said, 'repent,' he meant that the entire life of believers should be one of repentance," he gave a gift to us all, for he cast a glorious light upon the blessed path to close communion with our Triune God. *Winter Light* modeled that life of repentance with a ruthless beauty and searching vulnerability that I find rare in Christian authors. Because Bruce Ray Smith found God's searching grace a holy gift (Acts 5:31), I was encouraged as a reader to do the same. He helped me to kiss the blade of God's convicting grace and pull it in. I have been significantly helped in my repentance and faith by this work. I am a thankful debtor to the author, a brother I have not met, but who has helped me "find the old paths, and walk in them."

Joe Novenson
Senior Teaching Pastor
Lookout Mountain Presbyterian Church
Lookout Mountain, GA

~

*B*rother Lawrence himself could well have written this story; and those of us who find strength, hope, and instruction in Brother Lawrence's words will find those same things here in the confessional words of Bruce Ray Smith.

Phyllis Tickle
Editor, Author, Playwright,
& Compiler of The Divine Hours
Millington, TN

CPSIA information can be obtained at www.ICGtesting.com
Printed in the USA
BVOW011230021211

277335BV00002B/23/P

9 780982 871584